A Spirit
of Living

Henri J. M. Nouwen

John S. Mogabgab, *Series Editor*

UPPER
ROOM BOOKS®
NASHVILLE

THE HENRI NOUWEN SPIRITUALITY SERIES
A Spirituality of Living
Copyright © 2011 The Henri Nouwen Legacy Trust.
All rights reserved.

The Upper Room Web site: www.upperroom.org.
The Henri Nouwen Society Web site: www.HenriNouwen.org.

Unless otherwise indicated, Scripture quotations are from *The New Jerusalem Bible*, copyright © 1985 by Darton, Longman & Todd, Ltd. and Doubleday, a division of Random House, Inc. Reprinted by permission.

Scripture quotations designated NRSV are taken from the *New Revised Standard Version Bible*, copyright © 1989, Division of Christian Education of the National Council of Churches of Christ in the United States of America. Used by permission. All rights reserved.

Cover and Interior Design: Sue Smith and Pearson & Co.
Cover art: Gogh, Vincent van (1888). *Men Unloading a Boat at Arles.*
Museo Thyssen-Bornemisza, Madrid, Spain / Art Resource, NY.
Photo on page 62 by Mary Ellen Kronstein. Used by permission.

Library of Congress Cataloging-in-Publication Data
Nouwen, Henri J. M.
A spirituality of living / by Henri J. M. Nouwen.
    p. cm. — (The Henri Nouwen spirituality series)
"Henri J.M. Nouwen's works cited"--P.
Includes bibliographical references (p.).
ISBN 978-0-8358-1088-3
1. Christian life--Catholic authors. I. Title.
BX2350.3.N6925 2012
248.4'82—dc23

                                                          2011036058

Printed in the United States of America

CONTENTS

About the Henri Nouwen Spirituality Series   *iv*

Preface   *v*

Acknowledgments   *x*

Discipline and Discipleship   13

Solitude   19

Community   32

Ministry   43

The River   53

Notes   58

Henri J. M. Nouwen's Works Cited   59

About Henri J. M. Nouwen   61

ABOUT THE HENRI NOUWEN SPIRITUALITY SERIES

HENRI NOUWEN sought the center of things. Never content to observe life from the sidelines, his approach to new experiences and relationships was full throttle. He looked at the world with the enthusiastic anticipation of a child, convinced that right in the midst of life he would find the God who loves us without conditions. Helping us recognize this God in the very fabric of our lives was the enduring passion of Henri's life and ministry.

The Henri Nouwen Spirituality Series embodies Henri's legacy of compassionate engagement with contemporary issues and concerns. Developed through a partnership between the Henri Nouwen Society and Upper Room Ministries, the Series offers fresh presentations of themes close to Henri's heart. We hope each volume will help you discover that in your daily round God is closer than you think.

PREFACE

THIS BOOK is coherent, compelling, and contains one of the most important teachings that Henri Nouwen ever gave. It is the fruit of Henri Nouwen's life as an academic, his deep engagement in the lives of countless people, his capacity for self-reflection, and his grounding in the life, spirit, and teaching of Jesus. It is not voluminous. While it probably did not take Henri a long time to write this text, it is the life wisdom of one of the spiritual masters of our time.

Each of us longs to live well, to experience love and belonging, to be connected to family and friends, and to make our unique contribution to others. But what path shall we take? What will lead us to the fulfillment of our deepest longings? In short, how shall we live? Henri offers us a spirituality that addresses these questions—a spirituality for living, a spirituality that has the potential to transform our lives.

I met Henri Nouwen in 1984 at Jean Vanier's L'Arche community in Trosly-Breuil, France. Henri was on a sabbatical from Harvard University, living in L'Arche, and I was a worker-assistant in the same community. We began a friendship that deepened over the next decade as we both assumed leadership within L'Arche.

I knew, of course, that Henri was a teacher and a writer; he had degrees in psychology and theology and had positions at prestigious universities. But I discovered that he was also a lifelong student of himself and others. Our personal friendship and work in the context of L'Arche gave me an unexpected glimpse into Henri's own exploration of life's most important questions. And I was an eyewitness to his deep listening to others—people from all walks of life, of diverse ethnic and religious backgrounds, both the weak and the strong.

Henri accompanied people who were falling in love and those who were grieving the loss of a failed relationship. He came close to and sat with people who were dying. He joyfully joined in the private and public celebrations of new birth. Henri listened deeply to people who were social justice activists and also to others who felt drawn to a more inner, contemplative way of living. Henri walked with people who were depressed and suicidal as well as those who were at the prime of their personal creativity. He was friends with people who had enormous wealth and those whose only wealth was the largesse of their hearts.

Through all of this Henri came to know the contours of the human heart.

Like others before him, Henri believed that our journey to become more fully human is a spiritual journey that begins and ends in the heart of God. And as a spiritual cartographer, he mapped out a path that we can follow.

In the following pages, Henri invites us to think about our lives in terms of three inter-connected "moments" that he sees modeled in the life of Jesus: solitude, community, and compassionate service to others. It is through solitude and prayer that we can stay in touch with our truest identity as children of God. This leads us into relationships with others in community where we learn to celebrate and forgive. Then, it is these relationships that sustain us as we reach out to serve others through compassionate ministry.

Henri's deepest longings were touched as he made the choice to enter into this cycle of solitude, community, and compassionate ministry. He offers this path to us, convinced that it will be fruitful for you and me.

Henri is a credible guide. He "walked the talk" of this spirituality throughout his life. He fought "demons" along his own journey and stood with others as they fought their demons. He learned not to be afraid of suffering—his own, that of others, or the suffering of the world.

Above all, Henri strove to live a faithful life. He wanted to be faithful to God, to his own unique gifts, to his community, and to the cry of suffering he heard all around him. His spiritual vision for living is grounded in his desire to live in the truth of his life. Is that not the aspiration of us all?

By entering into solitude, engaging others in relationship, and reaching into the suffering of the world with compassion, Henri found his truth. He also found a peace that passes understanding.

This book will guide us to that same place.

Nathan Ball

The Henri Nouwen Legacy Trust

ACKNOWLEDGMENTS

THE FURTHER an editor advances in a publishing series, the more appreciation he or she must have for the support team that accompanies the appearance of each new volume. Certainly that is true for the book you are holding. Its winsome proportions and open design are due to the creative energies of Resa Pearson and Elaine Go of Pearson and Company in Santa Clara, California. Designer Nelson Kane burnished the cover to achieve its luminous vitality. Access to the manuscripts from which this one draws its substance would have been considerably more time-consuming were it not for the generous assistance of Gabrielle Earnshaw, careful steward of the Henri Nouwen Archives at the University of St. Michael's College in Toronto. Safe passage of the content through the land of rights and permissions would have been more difficult save for the expert advice and detailed research of Kathryn Smith at the Henri Nouwen

Legacy Trust. Her editorial suggestions and those of Trustees Sue Mosteller and Nathan Ball have strengthened the text in numerous ways. Special gratitude belongs to Nathan for making time in a fearsome schedule to write the Preface.

Dependable as always, my colleagues at Upper Room Books kept the project on the front burner of my priorities when distractions led me astray. Eli Fisher's sharp editorial eye, Rita Collett's project management genius, and Nanci Lamar's production expertise all helped a manuscript become a book. Robin Pippin, formerly editorial director of Upper Room Books and now associate executive director of publishing at Upper Room Ministries, has surrounded the project with calm confidence and unstinting support.

John S. Mogabgab
Series Editor

A cloud came, covering them in shadow; and from the cloud there came a voice, "This is my Son, the Beloved. Listen to him."

(Mark 9:7)

Discipline
and
Discipleship

A spiritual life
without discipline
is impossible.

—*Making All Things New*

THE SPIRITUAL life is a life that is guided by God's Spirit, the same Spirit that guided the life of Jesus. So how can we be in touch with the Spirit, hear the voice of the Spirit, and allow ourselves to be guided by the Spirit? This is not so easy in a world where there are so many things going on and so many voices calling for our attention. Can we create some space for God where we can hear, feel, experience the Spirit of God, and where it becomes possible for us to respond? Is there space in our lives where the Spirit of God has a chance of getting our attention?

It is the Holy Spirit who offers us the life that death cannot destroy.

—Bread for the Journey

Our lives are full. There are things to do, people to meet, activities to pursue. We want to be fully occupied, to know that because we are busy people something important is happening in our lives. And if we are not occupied then we are at least preoccupied—filled with concern about things that have not yet come about or have already come about. We fill our inner space with worry about things that might happen and guilt about things that have already happened. And beneath our worry and our guilt there is a deep fear of empty spaces. When we create an empty space, we make room for something to happen to us that we cannot predict, something that might be really new and lead us to places we would rather not go (John 21:15-19). This is where discipline in the spiritual life becomes important.

The word *discipleship* and the word *discipline* are the same word—that has always fascinated me. Once we have made the choice to say, "Yes, I want to follow Jesus," the question is, "What disciplines will help me remain faithful to that choice?" If we want to be disciples of Jesus, we have to live a disciplined life.

By discipline, I do not mean control. If I know the discipline of psychology or of economics, I have a certain control over a body of

It requires real discipline to let God and not the world be the Lord of our mind.

—Here and Now

knowledge. If I discipline my children, I want to have a little control over them. But in the spiritual life, the word discipline means "the effort to create some space in which God can act." Discipline means to prevent everything in our life from being filled up. Discipline means that somewhere we're not occupied, and certainly not preoccupied. In the spiritual life, discipline means to create that space in which something can happen that we hadn't planned or counted on. Discipline helps us to follow the voice of the Spirit, who wants to lead us to new places, new people, and new forms of service.

I think three disciplines are important for us to remain faithful so we not only become disciples but also remain disciples. These disciplines are contained in one passage from Scripture with which we're familiar, but one that we may be surprised to find speaks about discipline.

Now it happened in those days that he went onto the mountain to pray; and he spent the whole night in prayer to God. When day came he summoned his disciples and picked out twelve of them; he called them 'apostles': Simon whom he called Peter, and his brother Andrew, James, John, Philip, Bartholomew, Matthew, Thomas, James son of Alphaeus, Simon called the Zealot, Judas son of James, and Judas Iscariot who became a traitor.

He then came down with them and stopped at a piece of level ground where there was a large gathering of his disciples, with a great crowd of people from all parts of Judaea and Jerusalem and the coastal region of Tyre and Sidon who had come to hear him and be cured of their diseases. People tormented by unclean spirits were also cured, and everyone in the crowd was trying to touch him because power came out of him that cured them all (Luke 6:12–19).

This is a beautiful story that moves from night to morning to afternoon. Jesus spent the night in solitude with God. In the morning, he gathered his apostles around him and formed community. In the afternoon, with his apostles, he went out and preached the Word and healed the sick. Notice the order—from solitude to community to ministry. The night is for solitude; the morning for community; the afternoon for ministry.

So often in ministry, I have wanted to do it by myself. If it didn't work, I went to others and said, "Please!" searching for a community to help me. If that didn't work, maybe I'd start praying. But the order that Jesus teaches us is the reverse. It begins by being with God in solitude; then it creates a fellowship, a community of people with whom we are living the mission; and finally this community goes out together to heal and to proclaim the Good News.

When I knew I was walking with the Lord, I always felt happy and at peace.

—¡Gracias!

I believe we can look at solitude, community, and ministry as three disciplines by which we create space for God. If we create space in which God can act and speak, something surprising will happen. You and I are called to these disciplines if we want to be disciples.

Solitude

In solitude we not only
encounter God but also
our true self.

—*Clowning in Rome*

S OLITUDE IS being with God and God alone. Is there a space for that in our lives?

COMMUNION

In every human heart there lives a deep hunger for communion. This hunger manifests itself in many ways: in a desire to be held; in a need to be close to someone; in a search for intimacy, friendship, and companionship; in the hope of being listened to and understood; in a craving for union of body, mind, and heart. The hunger for communion is never far away from us. Whenever it is satisfied, we experience joy and peace. Whenever it is frustrated, we experience pain and, often, inner anguish. We want to belong, to be connected, to feel at home, to be safe, and we can fulfill none of these desires on our own. Our whole being yearns for another mind; our heart needs another heart.

Communion creates community, because the God living in us makes us recognize the God in our fellow humans.

—With Burning Hearts

Our deep hunger for communion is a precious gift from God and a true driving force of our spiritual journey. Our hunger for communion is the source of our faith, our hope, and our love. It is also the source of our unbelief, our despair, and our fear. The way we live with our hunger for communion is the decisive factor in our lives.

To believe in Jesus means to believe in the communion that exists between Jesus and the Father. Jesus asks, "Do you believe in me?" (see John 11:25-26). By that he means, "Do you believe I am the one who is in full communion with God? Do you believe that all that the Father says to me I say to you? Do you believe that all the works the Father wants to do he does through me? Do you believe that I am the one who is sent by the Father?" To believe in Jesus is to believe in Jesus as the one who is sent by God and in whom God's fullness becomes visible. And if you take it one step further, to believe in Jesus means to believe in the intimate, full, total communion between the Father and the Son, that seeing Jesus is seeing the Father, touching Jesus is touching God, God who is father, mother, brother, sister. And Jesus wants to include us in this most intimate communion by giving us the Holy Spirit: "It is good that I go," says Jesus, "so that I can send you the Spirit" (see John 16:7). In and through the Spirit we become full participants in the communion of love that Jesus shares with his Father. That is the mystery of our redemption and the promise of the spiritual life.

LISTENING

Jesus spent the whole night in communion. The way I would like to define communion here is that Jesus spent the night listening to the Father calling him the Beloved. That is the voice Jesus heard when he came up out of the Jordan River (Luke 3:22), and he hears that same voice on the mountain: "You are my beloved Son, on you my favor rests. I declare you to be my Beloved, the one in whom I pour out all my love. You are my favorite one" (see Luke 9:35). It is with this knowledge of being the Beloved that Jesus could walk freely into a world in which he was not treated as the Beloved. People applauded him, laughed at him, praised him, and rejected him. They called out "Hosanna!" and they called out "Crucify!" But in the midst of all those voices, Jesus knew one thing—*I am the Beloved; I am God's favorite one*. He clung to that voice. When Jesus enters into prayer in the night he is totally free from everything and totally open to the voice that calls him the Beloved.

Why is it so important that we are with God and God alone on the mountaintop? It's important because it's the place in which we can listen to the voice of the One who calls us the beloved. Jesus says to you and to me that we are loved as he is loved. That same voice is there for us. To pray is to let that voice speak to the center of our being and permeate our whole life. Who am I? I am the beloved. If we are not claiming that voice as the deepest truth of our being, then we cannot walk freely in this world.

In the world there are many other voices speaking—loudly: "Prove that you are the beloved. Prove you're worth something. Prove you have any contribution to make. Do something relevant. Be sure you make a name for yourself. At least have some power—then people will love you; then people will say you're wonderful, you're great."

Secularity is a way of being dependent on the responses of our milieu.

—The Way of the Heart

These voices are so strong. They touch our hidden insecurities and drive us to become very busy trying to prove to the world that we are good people who deserve some attention. Sometimes we think that our busyness is just an expression of our vocation, but Jesus knew that often our attempts to prove our worth are an example of temptation. Right after Jesus heard the voice say, "You are my Beloved," another voice said, "Prove you are the Beloved. Do something. Change these stones into bread. Be sure you're famous. Jump from the Temple, and you will be known. Grab some power so you have real influence. Don't you want some influence? Isn't that why you came?"

Jesus said, "No, I don't have to prove anything. I am already the Beloved" (Matt. 4:1-11).

I love Rembrandt's painting *The Return of the Prodigal Son.* The father holds his child, touches his child, and says, "You are my beloved. I'm not going to ask you any questions. Wherever you have gone, whatever you have done, and whatever people say about you, you're my beloved. I hold you safe in my embrace. You can come home to me whose name is Compassionate, whose name is Love."

If we keep that in mind, we can deal with an enormous amount of success as well as an enormous amount of failure without losing our

God does not require a pure heart before embracing us.

—The Road to Daybreak

identity, because our identity is that we are the beloved. Long before our father and mother, our brothers and sisters, our teachers, our church, or anyone else touched us in a loving or a wounding way—long before we were rejected by some person or praised by somebody else—that voice was there. "I have loved you with an everlasting love" (Jer. 31:3). That love was there before we were born and will be there after we die. A life of fifty, sixty, seventy, or a hundred years is just a little moment in which we have been given time to say, "Yes, I love you too." God has become so vulnerable, so little, so dependent in a manger and on a cross and is asking us again and again, "Do you love me? Do you really love me?"

This listening is not easy. Jesus spent the *night* in prayer. That is an image of the fact that prayer is not something we always feel. God's voice is not a voice we always hear with physical ears. God's word is not always an insight that suddenly comes to us in our minds or that satisfies our hearts. God's heart is greater than the human heart and therefore transcends our feelings and emotions. God's mind is greater than the human mind and therefore transcends our insights and good ideas. Much real prayer of communion takes place in the night, in the night of faith, in the darkness that comes upon us because the light of God is so great that it blinds us and makes our heart and mind unable to grasp what we are learning.

That is where the discipline of prayer comes in. We are called to pray not because we feel like praying or because it gives us great insights, but simply because we want to be obedient, to listen to the voice that calls us the beloved. The word *listen* in Latin is *audire*. If we listen with full attention in which we are totally geared to listen, it's called *ob-audire*, and that's where the word *obedience* comes from. Jesus is the obedient one. That means he is total ear, totally open to the love of God. And if we are closed, and to the degree that we are closed, we are *surdus*. That is the Latin word for *deaf*. The more "deaf" we get, the more *absurdus* we become, and an absurd life is precisely a life in which we no longer listen and are constantly distracted by all sorts of voices and lose touch with the truth that we are the beloved. And as soon as we start to become spiritually deaf to the voice that calls us the beloved, we are going to look someplace else to make us the beloved. And that's when we get into trouble.

Prayer brings love alive among us.

—¡Gracias!

We are going to look for love, affirmation, or praise where we cannot find them and get hooked in all sorts of ways, whether it is alcohol, drugs, relationships, success in work, how people talk about us, or desire to have control over things.

Real freedom to live in this world comes from hearing clearly the truth about who we are, which is that we are the beloved. That's what prayer is about. And that's why it is so crucial and not just a nice thing to do once in a while. It is the essential attitude that creates in us the freedom to love other people not because they are going to love us back but because we are so loved and out of the abundance of that love we want to give.

This is where ministry starts, because our freedom is anchored in claiming our belovedness. Being the beloved allows us to go into this world and touch people, heal them, speak with them, and make them aware that they too are beloved, chosen, and blessed. When we discover our belovedness, we begin to see the belovedness of other people and call that forth. It is an incredible mystery of God's love that the more we know how deeply we are loved, the more we will see how deeply our sisters and our brothers in the human family are loved.

But we have to pray. We have to listen to the voice that calls us the beloved.

Oh, if we could sit for just one half hour a day doing nothing except taking a simple word or phrase from the Bible and holding it in our heart and mind. "The LORD is my shepherd;

I shall not want" (Ps. 23:1, NRSV). Say it three times. We know it's not true, because we want many things. That is exactly why we're so nervous. But if we keep saying the truth, the real truth—"The LORD is my shepherd; I shall not want"—and let that truth descend from our minds into our hearts, gradually those words will be written on the walls of our inner holy place. That becomes the space in which we can receive our colleagues and our work, our family and our friends, and the people we will meet during the day.

Why, O Lord, is it so hard for me to keep my heart directed toward you?

—A Cry for Mercy

The trouble is that as soon as we sit and become quiet, we think, *Oh, I forgot this. I should call my friend. Later on I'm going to see him.* Our inner life is like a banana tree filled with monkeys jumping up and down. It is not easy to sit and trust that in solitude God will speak to us—not as a magical voice but as knowledge that grows gradually over the years. And in that word from God we will find the inner place from which to live our lives.

Solitude is where Jesus listened to God. It is where we listen to God. Solitude is where community begins.

Community

Community is where
humility and glory touch.

—*Bread for the Journey*

IT IS precisely in communion with God through prayer that we discover the call to community. It is remarkable that solitude always calls us to community. In solitude we realize we are part of a human family and that we want to live something together.

By community, I don't mean formal communities. I mean families, friends, parishes, Twelve-Step programs, prayer groups. Community is not an organization; community is a way of living. We gather around us people with whom we want to proclaim the truth that we are the beloved sons and daughters of God.

Community is not easy. Parker Palmer once observed that community is the "place where the person you least want to live with always lives."[1] In Jesus' community of twelve disciples, the last name was that of someone who was going to betray him (Luke 6:13-16). That person is always in our community somewhere. In the eyes of others, we might be that person.

I live in a community called Daybreak—one of over a hundred communities throughout the world where children, men, and women with intellectual disabilities and those who assist them live together. We share all aspects of day-to-day living. Nathan, Janet, and all the other people of our community know how hard it is and how beautiful it is to live together.

Why is it so important that solitude come before community? If we do not know we are the beloved sons and daughters of God, we are going to expect someone in the community to make us feel that we are. We will expect someone to give us that perfect, unconditional love. They cannot. Often this means a painfully temporary quality in our relationships. Instead of long-lasting involvements that grow stronger over time, we may experience ruptures, separations, and growing despair about finding someone who can meet our deepest desires for intimacy. How quickly anticipation can give way to exhaustion and even depression as we search for anyone who can take away our loneliness.

Wherever we look we see lonely people. Maybe the main source of human suffering in contemporary western society is loneliness. Children wander about alone in the streets of big cities. Teenagers often feel so alone that they look to drugs or sex for momentary relief. Young adults experience isolation in their work and often in their own homes. Everywhere there are people who suffer from silence in their relationships, fear in their reaching out to others, pain in their moments of intimacy, and anguish in times of absence and loss. Much of what we see on television, hear on the radio, and read in the newspapers is about stories of separation, jealousy, suspicion, rivalry, violence, war, and destruction. It seems that our whole human family is ripped apart and suffering from abysmal loneliness. And underneath all of this is the weeping—the weeping of the human heart aching for community.

Community is not loneliness grabbing onto loneliness: "I'm so lonely; you're so lonely. Please stay awhile!" Grabbing too easily becomes grasping, and grasping may quickly turn into suffocating closeness. No, community is solitude greeting solitude: "I am the beloved; you are the beloved. Together we can build a home." Sometimes we are close to each other, and that's wonderful. Sometimes we don't feel much love, and that's hard. But we can be faithful. We can build a home together and create space for God and for the children of God.

To live a spiritual life we must first find the courage to enter into the desert of our loneliness and to change it by gentle and persistent efforts into a garden of solitude.

—Reaching Out

Within the discipline of community are the disciplines of forgiveness and celebration. Forgiveness and celebration are what make marriage, friendship, or any other form of community possible.

FORGIVENESS

What is forgiveness? Forgiveness is to allow the other person not to be God. Forgiveness says, "I know you love me, but you don't have to love me unconditionally, because no human being can do that."

We all have wounds. We all are in so much pain. It is precisely a feeling of loneliness that lurks behind all our successes, a feeling of uselessness that hides under all the praise we receive, a feeling of meaninglessness even when people say we are fantastic that makes us sometimes grab onto people and expect from them an affection and love they cannot give.

By not forgiving, I chain myself to a desire to get even, thereby losing my freedom.

—The Road to Daybreak

If we want other people to give us something that only God can give, we become a heavy burden. We say, "Love me!" and before we know it we become demanding and manipulative and maybe even violent. It is so important that we keep forgiving one another—not once in a while, but every moment. Before we have had our breakfast, we have already had at least three opportunities to forgive people, because our mind is already wondering: *What will they think about me? What will he or she do? How will they use me?*

To forgive other people for being able to give us only a little love—that is a hard discipline. To keep asking others for forgiveness because we can give only a little love—that is a hard discipline, too. It hurts to say to our children, to our wife or our husband, to our friends, that we cannot give them all we would like to give. And it is a hard discipline to offer forgiveness to others even when they are not able to receive that forgiveness. Still, offering and receiving forgiveness is where community begins to be created. Community forms when we come together in a forgiving and undemanding way.

CELEBRATION

This is where celebration, the second discipline of community, comes in. "Celebration," writes Jean Vanier, "nourishes us, restores hope and brings us the strength to live with the sufferings and difficulties of everyday life."[2] If we can forgive that another person cannot give us what only God can give, then we can celebrate that person's gift. Then we can see the love that person is giving us as a reflection of God's great, unconditional love. Our relationships are endlessly varied because God's love is inexhaustible and can be made visible in countless ways. What is important is that we know that it is God who calls us together. "Love one another, as I have loved you" (John 15:12). When we know that first love, we can see the love that comes to us from people as a reflection of it. This knowledge allows us to live through many hard times and hard moments. We can celebrate that love and say, "That's beautiful!"

In our community, Daybreak, we have to do a lot of forgiving. But right in the midst of forgiving comes celebrating: We see

Through celebration we enter into the Kingdom of Heaven.

—Creative Ministry

the beauty of people whom society quite often considers marginal. With forgiveness and celebration, community becomes the place where we call forth the gifts of other people, lift them up, and say, "You are the beloved daughter and the beloved son."

To celebrate another person's gift doesn't mean giving each other little compliments— "You play the piano better"; "You are so good at singing." No, that's a talent show. To celebrate each other's gifts means to accept each other's humanity. At Daybreak we see each other as people who can smile, say "Welcome," eat, and take a few steps. People who in the eyes of others are broken suddenly are full of life, because we discover our own brokenness through them.

Here is what I mean. In this world, so many people live with the burden of self-rejection: *I'm not good. I'm useless. People don't really care for me. If I didn't have money, they wouldn't talk to me. If I didn't have this big job, they wouldn't call me. If I didn't have this influence, they wouldn't love me.* Beneath many successful and highly praised careers can live fearful people who do not think much of themselves. They are living divided lives and feel they must keep their inner reality hidden from those who know only their outer impression. They are living isolated lives, cut off from others because they believe that their value lies only in the gifts they have to offer and not also in the gifts they can receive. In community we are leaders from the place of our gifts and followers from the place of other people's gifts. Community cultivates that mutual vulnerability in which we forgive each other and celebrate each other's gifts.

One of the greatest dangers in the spiritual life is self-rejection.

—Bread for the Journey

I have learned so much since coming to Daybreak. I have learned that my real gifts are not that I write books or that I taught at universities. My real gifts are discovered by Janet and Nathan and others, who know me so well they cannot be impressed any more by these things. Once in a while they say, "I have good advice: Why don't you read some of your own books?"

There is healing in being known in my vulnerability and impatience and weakness. Suddenly I realize that I am a good person also in the eyes of people who don't read books and who don't care about success. These people can forgive me constantly for the little egocentric gestures and behaviors that are always there.

Ministry

Jesus calls us to continue his
mission of revealing
the perfect love of God
in this world.

—*The Road to Daybreak*

ALL DISCIPLES of Jesus are called to ministry. Ministry is not, first of all, something that we do (although it calls us to do many things). Ministry is something that we have to trust. If we know we are the beloved, and if we keep forgiving those with whom we form community and celebrate their gifts, we cannot do other than minister.

Jesus did not cure people by doing all sorts of complicated things. He did not say, "Let me talk to you for ten minutes, and maybe I can do something about this." Rather, a power went out from his pure heart and people were cured. He wanted one thing—to do the will of God. He was the completely obedient one, the one who was always listening to God. Out of this listening came an intimacy with God that radiated out to everyone Jesus saw and touched.

Ministry means we have to trust that. We have to trust that if we are the son or daughter of God, power will go out from us and people will be healed.

"Go out and heal the sick. Walk on the snake. Call the dead to life." This is not small talk. Yet Jesus said, "In all truth I tell you, whoever believes in me will perform the same works as I do myself, and will perform even greater works" (John 14:12). Jesus wanted his disciples then and now to understand that we are sent into the world just as he was sent into the world—to heal, to cure, and to proclaim the Good News (see Luke 9:1-2).

Trust in that healing power. Trust that if we are living as the beloved we will heal people whether or not we are aware of it. But we have to be faithful to that call.

Healing ministry can be expressed through two disciplines: gratitude and compassion.

We will exercise true power and walk through this valley of darkness performing and witnessing miracles.

—Finding My Way Home

GRATITUDE

Healing often happens by leading people to gratitude, because the world is full of resentment.

What is resentment? It is cold anger. *I'm angry with him. I'm angry at this situation. This is not the way I want it.* We tend to divide our past into good things to remember with gratitude and painful things to accept or reject. Once we accept this division, however, we quickly develop a mentality in which we hope to collect more good memories than bad memories, more things to be grateful for than things to be resentful about, more things to celebrate than to complain about.

Nothing is as difficult as really accepting one's own life.

—Creative Ministry

But our lives are full of losses—losses of dreams and losses of friends and losses of family and losses of hopes. Over time, there are more and more things we can be negative about. Resentment makes us cling to our failures or disappointments and complain about the losses in our lives. There is always a lurking danger that we will respond to life's incredible pains with resentment. Resentment gives us a hardened heart and we become resentful people.

Gratitude in its deepest sense means to live life as a gift to be received gratefully. But gratitude as the gospel speaks about it embraces *all* of life: the good and the bad, the joyful and the painful, the holy and the not so holy. Is it truly possible to embrace with gratitude all of our life and not just the good things that we like to remember?

Jesus calls us to gratitude. He calls us to recognize that gladness and sadness are never separate, that joy and sorrow really belong together, and that mourning and dancing are part of the same movement. That is why Jesus calls us to be grateful for every moment that we have lived and to claim our unique journey as God's way to mold our hearts to greater conformity with God's own. The cross is the main symbol of our faith, and it invites us to find hope where we see pain and to reaffirm the resurrection where we see death. The call to be grateful is a call to trust

> *Gratitude needs to be discovered and to be lived with great inner attentiveness.*
>
> —With Burning Hearts

that every moment of our life can be claimed as the way of the cross that leads us to new life. Can we be grateful for everything that has happened in our life—not just the good things but for all that has brought us to today?

In this world's eyes, there is an enormous distinction between good times and bad, between sorrow and joy. But in the eyes of God, they are never separated. Our ministry is to help people gradually let go of their resentment and discover that right in the middle of suffering there is a blessing. Where there is pain, there is healing. Where there is mourning, there is dancing. Where there is poverty, there is the Kingdom of God.

Gratitude belongs to the core of the life of Jesus and his followers.

—Lifesigns

Jesus says to us, "Cry over your pains, and you will discover that I'm right there in your tears, and you will be grateful for my presence in your weakness." Ministry means to help people become grateful for life even with pain.

Gratitude can lead us into the world precisely to the places where people are in pain. Sometimes that pain is hidden in a person who from the outside seems to be without pain or looks successful. The minister, the disciple of Jesus, goes where there is pain not because he is a masochist or she is a sadist, but because God is hidden in the pain.[3]

COMPASSION

Compassion means to suffer with, to live with those who suffer. When Jesus saw the woman of Nain he realized, *This is a widow who has lost her only son*, and he was moved by compassion. He felt the pain of that woman in his guts. He felt her pain so deeply in his spirit that out of compassion he called the son to life so he could give that son back to his mother (Luke 7:11-15).

Compassion means full immersion in the condition of being human.

—Compassion

The Dutch painter Vincent van Gogh felt similar pain when he lived in solidarity with the poor in the bleak mining district of Belgium or painted with compassionate brush strokes the portraits of hungry peasants in South Holland. He wanted to reach the deep, hidden human sorrow and bring it to the surface to be seen, not so as to frighten us, but to console.

Consolation is the deepening of a pain to a level where it can be shared. For Vincent, joy and sorrow are mysteriously related and can never be fully separated. To express both gladness and sorrow, both light and dark, both the joy of living and the pain of dying: that was his consoling task. His artistic work was an uninterrupted struggle to reach the hearts of people and their worlds. Through his sketches, drawings, and paintings, van Gogh shows us that solidarity in suffering, even when this calls for a deepening of the pain to a level where real sharing is possible, leads not to commiseration but to "comfort," which means new "strength together."[4]

Blessed are those who embrace each other in weakness, because they will possess the land. They will experience new begin-nings. When we take the great human risk of compassion, of suffering together, and when we dare to face with each other our dreadful loneli-ness, then new life starts becoming manifest.

The blessed one always blesses.

—Life of the Beloved

As disciples of Jesus, we are sent to wher-ever there is poverty, loneliness, suffering of any kind. We are given the courage to be with suf-fering people. We can trust that by entering into places of pain, we will find the joy of Jesus. A new world grows out of compassion.

The call to compassionate ministry is a great call. But we must not be fearful. We must not say, "I can't do that." When we are aware that we are the beloved, and when we have friends around us with whom we live in community, we can do anything. We're not afraid anymore. We're not afraid to knock on the door while somebody is dying. We're not afraid to open a discussion with a person who underneath all the glitter is much in need of ministry. We're free.

I have experienced that constantly. When I was depressed or when I felt anxious, I knew my friends couldn't solve it. Those who ministered to me were those who were not afraid to be with me. Precisely where I felt my poverty, I discovered God's blessing.

The River

Fruitfulness in the spiritual
life is about love.

—Finding My Way Home

J UST A few weeks ago a friend of mine died. He was a classmate, and they sent me the tape of his funeral service. The first reading in that service was a story about a little river. The little river said, "I can become a big river." It worked hard, but there was a big rock. The river said, "I'm going to get around this rock." The little river pushed and pushed, and since it had a lot of strength, it got itself around the rock.

Soon the river faced a big wall, and the river kept pushing this wall. Eventually, the river made a canyon and carved a way through. The growing river said, "I can do it. I can push it. I am not going to let down for anything."

Then there was an enormous forest. The river said, "I'll go ahead anyway and just force these trees down." And the river did.

The river, now powerful, stood on the edge of an enormous desert with the sun beating down. The river said, "I'm going to go through this desert." But the hot sand soon began to soak up the whole river. The river said, "Oh, no. I'm going to do it. I'm going to get myself through this desert." But the river soon had drained into the sand until it was only a small mud pool.

Then the river heard a voice from above: "Just surrender. Let me lift you up. Let me take over."

The river said, "Here I am."

The sun then lifted up the river and made the river into a huge cloud. He carried the river right over the desert and let the cloud rain down and make the fields far away fruitful and rich.

There is a moment in our lives when we stand before the desert and want to do it ourselves. But there is the voice that comes to us, "Let go. Surrender. In this parched land, I will make you fruitful. Yes, trust me. Give yourself to me."

What counts in your life and mine is not successes but fruits. The fruits of our life are born often in our pain and in our vulnerability and in our losses. The fruits of our life come only after the plow has carved through our land. God wants us to be fruitful.

Let's remind one another that what brings us true joy is not successfulness but fruitfulness.

—Bread for the Journey

The question is not, "How much can I still do in the years that are left to me?" The question is, "How can I prepare myself for total surrender so my life can be fruitful?"

Our little lives are small, human lives. But in the eyes of the One who calls us the beloved, we are great—greater than the years we have. We will bear fruit, fruit that you and I will not see on this earth but whose reality we can trust.

Solitude, community, ministry—these disciplines help us live a fruitful life. Remain in Jesus; he remains in you. You will bear many fruits, you will have great joy, and your joy will be complete.[5]

Remain in me, as I in you. As a branch cannot bear fruit all by itself, unless it remains part of the vine, neither can you unless you remain in me.

(John 15:4)

NOTES

1. Parker J. Palmer, *The Promise of Paradox: A Celebration of Contradictions in the Christian Life* (Notre Dame, Ind.: Ave Maria Press, 1980), 83.

2. Jean Vanier, *Community and Growth: Our Pilgrimage Together* (New York: Paulist Press, 1979), 200. Jean Vanier is the founder of L'Arche.

3. Some material in this section is from Henri Nouwen, "All Is Grace," *Weavings*, Vol. VII, No. 6 (November/December 1992), 39-40.

4. Some material in this paragraph is taken directly or adapted from an article originally published in *America* (March 13, 1976), 197-98.

5. In addition to materials identified in the above notes, this volume draws on the following sources from Henri Nouwen's literary legacy: "Moving From Solitude to Community to Ministry" (*Leadership* Magazine, Spring 1995); Transcript of "An Evening with Henri Nouwen" (St. James' Church, New York City, November 11, 1993); "Communion" (unpublished manuscript); Transcript of an informal presentation on prayer (Westminster Presbyterian Church, Nashville, Tennessee, February 10, 1991); "The Life in Faith" (unpublished manuscript).

HENRI J. M. NOUWEN'S WORKS CITED

Page 13: *Making All Things New* (1981), 66.

Page 14: *Bread for the Journey* (1997), May 18.

Page 15: *Here and Now* (1994), 71.

Page 18: *¡Gracias!* (1983), 151.

Page 19: *Clowning in Rome* (1979), 30.

Page 20: *With Burning Hearts* (1994), 75.

Page 24: *The Way of the Heart* (1981), 22.

Page 25: *The Road to Daybreak* (1988), 72.

Page 28: *¡Gracias!* (1983), 12.

Page 30: *A Cry for Mercy* (1981), 26.

Page 32: *Bread for the Journey* (1997), May 3.

Page 36: *Reaching Out* (1975), 22.

Page 37: *The Road to Daybreak* (1998), 68.

Page 40: *Creative Ministry* (1971), 108.

Page 41: *Bread for the Journey* (1997), January 10.

Page 43: *The Road to Daybreak* (1988), 159.

Page 45: *Finding My Way Home* (2001), 49.

Page 46: *Creative Ministry* (1971), 97.

Page 47: *With Burning Hearts* (1994), 93.

Page 48: *Lifesigns* (1986), 56.

Page 49: *Compassion* (1982), 4.

Page 51: *Life of the Beloved* (1992), 67.

Page 53: *Finding My Way Home* (2001), 142-44.

Page 56: *Bread for the Journey* (1997), January 4.

ABOUT HENRI J. M. NOUWEN

Mary Ellen Kronstein

Henri Nouwen and John Mogabgab at Notre Dame in 1978

INTERNATIONALLY RENOWNED author, respected professor, and beloved pastor, Henri Nouwen wrote over forty books on the spiritual life that have inspired and comforted countless people throughout the world. Since his death in 1996, an ever-increasing number of readers, writers, and researchers are exploring his literary legacy. Henri Nouwen's works have been translated and published in more than twenty-two different languages.

Born in Nijkerk, Holland on January 24, 1932, Nouwen was ordained in 1957. Moved by his desire for a better understanding of human suffering, he went in 1964 to the United States to study in the Religion and Psychiatry Program at the Menninger Clinic. He went on to teach at the University of Notre Dame, the Pastoral Institute in Amsterdam, and the Divinity Schools of both Yale and Harvard, where his classes were among the most popular on campus.

His strong appeal as a teacher and writer had much to do with his passion to integrate all aspects of his life into a lived spirituality. Nouwen was convinced that striving for such integration is an urgent need in our culture. His writing, often autobiographical, has given readers a window into the joys and struggles of their own spiritual quest. The universal character of Nouwen's spiritual vision has crossed many boundaries and inspired a wide range of individuals: Wall Street bankers, politicians and professionals, Peruvian peasants, teachers, religious leaders, ministers and caregivers.

Nouwen traveled widely during his lifetime, lecturing on topics such as ministry and care-giving, compassion, peacemaking, suffering, solitude, community, dying, and death.

Nouwen was always searching for new images to convey the depth of the good news of the gospel message. For example, Henri met and befriended a group of trapeze artists in a traveling circus. Just prior to his sudden death, he was working on a project to use life in the circus as an image of the spiritual journey. *The Return of the Prodigal Son*, one of his classic works, marries art and spirituality in a contemporary interpretation of the ancient Gospel parable.

Henri lived the last ten years of his life with people who have developmental disabilities in a L'Arche community near Toronto, Canada.

Inspired by Henri Nouwen's conviction that one's personal relationship with God is the foundation for all other relationships, the Henri Nouwen Society exists to create opportunities and resources that support people in their desire to grow spiritually.